DUNSTANBURGH

Published 2004
by

Smokestack Books
PO Box 408, Middlesbrough TS5 6WA
Tel : 01642 813997
e-mail : info@smokestack-books.co.uk
www.smokestack-books.co.uk

Cover photo and photo on page 3 by Andrew Watchorn
Photo on page 43 by the author
Photo of author by Grant Sonnex

Cover design and print by
Archetype Tel: 0870 2245 151
www.archetype-uk.com

ISBN 0-9548691-1-7

Smokestack Books
gratefully acknowledges the support of
Middlesbrough Borough Council
and Arts Council North East.

Smokestack Books is a member of
The Independent Northern Publishers
www.northernpublishers.co.uk

DUNSTANBURGH

A radio-poem

Katrina Porteous

Acknowledgements

Dunstanburgh was commissioned by BBC Radio 4 and first broadcast on 9th February 2004 as *Dunstanburgh Castle – a Secret as Old as the Stones.* The producer was Julian May. My thanks to him and to everyone who was involved in the broadcast, especially actor Trevor Fox, and Mrs Ayden and the children of Seahouses First School. Thanks to English Heritage for access to the castle, to custodian Archie Turnbull, to Alistair Oswald and the English Heritage Landscape Investigation Team and to National Trust Archaeologist Harry Beamish. Special thanks to my friend Eve Foster, who encouraged the project from the beginning.

I am grateful to the Arts Foundation for an award which supported me during the research and writing of this poem.

Introduction

Dunstanburgh was written, not for the page, but for radio. It is a secret history, expressed through the sounds of the place itself. In reproducing the poem for the page, I have tried not to compromise its essentially aural nature. All poetry is meant to be heard out loud; but there are some aspects of poetry which radio is particularly well-equipped to serve, and it is these which I have tried to explore in this poem.

All my life, I have loved Dunstanburgh Castle on the Northumberland coast. I live almost within sight of it, in my grandparents' house, and one of my earliest memories is of gazing at its stark, ruined outline across the sea. In my early 20s, I spent a year visiting the castle several times a week in all weathers, to record in minute detail its natural, seasonal changes. This was my apprenticeship as a writer, learning to listen, and to lose myself in a place.

The castle was begun in 1313 by Thomas, Earl of Lancaster, who, recent research suggests, might have intended it partly as an advertisement for his own 'good lordship' – his powers of patronage and influence – perhaps even to rival those of the king. References to King Arthur seem implicit in Dunstanburgh's location and design. The castle was later altered by John of Gaunt, himself a baron with Arthurian pretensions; and it repeatedly served as a refuge for the local community during raids by the Scots.

It was during the Wars of the Roses that the first written reference occurred to Dunstanburgh's best-known legend, the story of the Seeker. A knight visiting the castle finds a girl trapped in the rock and, given the choice between a bugle and a sword to free her, chooses the bugle. He is then doomed to search for her forever. This story had strong political overtones in medieval times: during the reign of Henry VI, the king's failure to provide the ultimate 'good lordship' – his misuse of patronage and his failure to wield political power (the sword) – led to a breakdown of law and order which resulted in civil war and regicide. Dunstanburgh, one of Henry and his wife Margarets' strongholds, became a ruin: a reminder of the ideals for which it stood, which were never realised.

How was I to explore these themes in a poem? My starting-point was to return to the place and its sounds. Revisiting it over the course of last year to observe and write, I used a small tape machine to record what I heard – the sea, the wind, the birds on the cliffs, all the changing music of the year. I then used these sounds as the germ of the poem. The original script for *Dunstanburgh* was crowded with production notes, detailed instructions for the incorporation of sounds, to create an almost abstract, musical composition. I have pared these instructions down to a minimum for the page, leaving only essential sounds which are not otherwise indicated in the poem. These actual sounds are marked in bold black italics.

Dunstanburgh is composed of a variety of voices. Rather than having a linear narrative, it is structured around a year at the castle, and is made up, like the place itself, of fragments. These include the songs and monologues of past human inhabitants, and the still more ancient, wild, elemental chants of the place itself. In the radio broadcast, produced by Julian May, the chants were performed by children from Seahouses First School, while all the other strands were shared between my voice and that of a male actor, reading the parts in various locations, inside and outside, around the ruins. Individual voices are not differentiated within the text, but to distinguish the different dimensions, the descriptive, present-day passages are printed in plain typeface, while the chants, songs and monologues are indicated in italics. Where the dominant voice is italicised, a chant may occasionally be aligned to the right of the page, to indicate the different speaker.

There is one other unusual feature of *Dunstanburgh* as a radio poem. At times two or even three voices may be heard simultaneously. Out loud, this gives the effect of hearing the words differently, even of losing them altogether in pure sound: the voices become, like history, almost opaque. This musical effect is impossible to reproduce in print. Where it is intended, the simultaneous voices are set out in parallel columns of text, with the second voice aligned to the right. Where three voices are heard simultaneously, the lines are stepped, to give a sense of the rhythmic, but otherwise chaotic, onward rush of sound. The rest is left to the reader's inner ear.

Guided by these voices, as if in a walk around the ruins, the reader gradually discovers the intimate, hidden history of Dunstanburgh Castle. This is an aspect of spoken poetry which particularly interests me, and one which I think radio serves especially well: it returns poetry to one of its most ancient functions – to explore, through the arguments of history, a common sense of who we are.

Katrina Porteous, 2004

DUNSTANBURGH

Mad kittiwakes on an echoey crag:

There is a castle by the sea
That no road leads to any more –

On the height of a cliff, the farthest edge
Of land, a wind-rucked field; a wall

And gatehouse, ruled across the sky;
A city, seen from miles away;

A promise, pledged in tall stone towers
That, more than battle, passing years,

Winter on winter of wind and rain,
Have battered down to a great ruin;

There's a secret as old
As the stones to unlock:
There's a riddle, a mystery
Trapped in the rock,
   In the rock,
   In the rock,
   In the rock,
   In the rock,
   In the rock.

Fade into kittiwakes, merging with them completely.

And nobody visiting listens or stays
Long enough to tell that the noise

Of the sea on the cliff-face does not cease,
Or to say when the swallows and gulls that roost

In its loud, rocky hollows are suddenly gone
To the tug of winter; and nobody sees

How, in its hours of solitude,
The ruin is endlessly reclaimed:

Loud sea and wind:

Rift of rock,
Buckle. Twist.
Black scar,
Wrench, ruck.
Cold stone
Crust, crack:

Grey-green lichen,
Brittle, prickly,
Boils and blisters,
Crusty, crackly
Moon-craters,
Pale and warty,
Witches' fingers,
Scabbed and scaly.

Crosswort, stitchwort,
Sea-spurrey, scurvy-grass,
Rest-harrow, meadow-rue,
Shepherd's purse and goose-grass;

Stonecrop, forget-me-not,
Lady's-smock and speedwell;
Mouse-eared chickweed,
Bird's foot trefoil;

Waregoose, wullymint,
Mullymac an' kittiwake,
Tommy noddy, cuddy duck,
Tudelum an' gormer.

Deed tides, big tides,
Wullymint an' mullymac,
Come, Jack, shine the lowe,
Days is gettin' longer.

Rift of rock,
Buckle. Twist.
Black scar,
Wrench, ruck.

Cold stone
Crust,

Crack!
Grey-green lichen,
Brittle, prickly,
Boils and blisters,
Crusty, crackly

Moon-craters,
Pale and warty,
Witches' fingers,
Scabbed and scaly.

Waregoose,
Wullymint,
Mullymac,
Kittiwake,

Tommy noddy,
Cuddy duck,
Tudelum,
Gormer.

The salt wind racks the grass and high
Cirrus; claws the rutted sea –

Cloud, field, ashlar – each
Surface scored with deep, oblique

Furrows, slant and dissonant;
Music, frozen in perfect silence,

An argument of stone and sky –
Between the things that stream away –

Tear, race, fly – and those that stand;
Between the marks of human hands

And marks of frost and tide and wind.

Scratched and slanted,
Flurried, ruffled,
Whipped, wealed,
Ridged and rippled,
Grooved, scarred,
Meshed, barred,
Acid-pitted,
Pocked and stippled:

Go sky,
Wind-blown
Cloud, sea.
Stay, stone.

Oven-red,
Sulphur-yellow,
Thunder-dark,
Flesh-sallow,

Wind-clawed,
Storm-driven,

Scratched
And slanted,
Flurried, ruffled,
Whipped, wealed,

Ridged and rippled,
Grooved,

Field-furrowed,
Cloud-riven,

Pigeon-grey,
Sky-blown,
Sea-swept
Sandstone.

Go sky,
Wind-blown
Cloud, sea.
Stay, stone.

Scarred,
Meshed,

Barred,
Acid-pitted,
Pocked
And stippled:

Stay, stone.
Fly, go,
Sea, sky,
Wind-blown.

Inside tower:

All day, all night, the wind explores
The gaps, the cracks. The stones resist.

As if it was searching for something lost,
The wind interrogates the walls.

Through arrow-slit, down parapet,
Round inaccessible, remote

Corners – a peaceful window-seat,
Marooned like something beyond the tide –

The wind inquires. Round battlements,
Up spiral stairs, through chambers, halls,

Brimful of voices, the way a shell
Fills with remembered sounds of the sea,

It pries. It probes.
The castle echoes:

It has become the wind's instrument.

It's an island of rock.
It's a dragon, asleep,
With a dinosaur back
And the tail of a beast.
    It's a beast,
    It's a beast,
    It's a beast,
    It's a beast,
    It's a beast.

Fade out kittiwakes.

Hanging Stones:
Who?
    A dozen
Basalt towers,
Faceless, frozen;
Iron-armoured,
Rust red,
Hacked, cracked,
Cold blood

Automata, black and blind,
Prehistory, glowering out,
They hold the tower aloft,
Offering it to the sky,
Lifting it up, cold hands
Raised in sacrifice
To sun and star and wind.

Wind that brings iron and timber,
Takes sons, brings strangers,
Wind that fans the fire's hunger –
    Whisper. Whisper. Who lives here?

What did he have on his mind,
The architect who planned
The hilt of a sword, stuck
In the spine of the rock –
What was he thinking of?

We know, hiss the stones.

Sudden skylark.

Build me a tower. Make it high,
Like a city set on top
Of a hill, let it be seen
Like a landmark for a ship,
Like a dagger in a fist,
Or like a claw, or like a crest,
Or like a warrior, one sprung
From the seed of standing stones,
Or like an angle-iron, strong,
Or like a snarl, a scowl, a frown,
Or like a riddle in the rock,
Or like a key without a lock,
Or like a head upon a block,
Or like a crown upon a king.

Find me a spring. Dig me a lake
To surround my tower. Make
A silver island of the mind.
Let it shiver in the wind,
That, like a meeting with a twin,
Or like a ghost beneath a glass,
Or like a mirror and a face,
Or like an echo from the past,
Like a lily, like a swan,
Like a vision or a dream,
You may read it as a sign,

The reflection of the stone
Like the pages of a book,
Like a sword fast in a rock,
Or like a key without a lock,
Or like the Isle of Avalon.

Sea. Kittiwakes, loud:

In the city of kittiwakes everyone's scolding
The comings and goings,
The restless arrivals,
Departures, the shuffling
To-ings and fro-ings;

With their clean yellow beaks,
Their iron-grey backs,
Salt-white breasts
And their wings dipped in darkness.

White wings of a kittiwake
Shear off the cliff
In a deep sickle dive
Into empty air
To soar, and circle.

And back comes the babble –
Peremptory cries
That rise to a higher, angrier echo –
Angular splashes against the slow
Undertone of the sea.

And he's back again,
To elaborate greetings:
Head-shaking,
Billing,
Fencing twin beaks,

Excitedly weaving two heads back and forward
While everyone shrieks,
And the entire city
Grinds into gear to announce the arrival.

A snowstorm of kittiwakes, shaken, won't settle,
In the shanty-town,
In the high-rise huddle,
The tenement squalor,
The squabble and babble.

There's a secret as old
As the stones to unlock:
There are bones in the soil –
Something sleeps in the rock.
> *In the rock,*
> *In the rock,*
> *In the rock,*
> *In the rock,*
> *In the rock.*

Kittiwakes swallow up this end, then fade out.

Hauled out like boats, the eider ducks
Warble and preen on the barnacled rocks.
There are sparkles sewn on the folds of the sea.

Far below, a metallic clatter:
A cormorant struggles out of the water,

Ungainly till airborne. Landlocked, another
Folds up his wings like an old, black umbrella.

On the scurvy-grass cliff-top, salt-white,
A fulmar peels, the blade of a knife,
From the rind of the black rock into the light;

And where the sea-pinks rustle their dresses,
Where the salt wind combs the grass,
A tatty sea, its shadow crosses

Over the edge, and by its straight
And soundless flight, the land is blessed.

Waregoose, wullymint,
Mullymac an' kittiwake,
Tommy noddy, cuddy duck,
Tudelum an' gormer.

Deed tides, big tides,
Wullymint an' mullymac,
Come, Jack, shine the lowe,
Days is gettin' longer.

Sea on rocks, echoey:

Bare Gull Crag sees little sun.
Wrinkled whinstone, ancient skin,

Scabbed and ring-wormed, brutal, alien,
Hunches down beneath the wind.

Cold rock. Musty blocks
Softened by the nap of a velvet moss,

Stained with streaks of rust and purple,
Iron-rich; burned autumnal

Fiery gold and salt-white crystal,
Compost-green and crimson mineral,

Feed the lichens' grey-green spores
On the prehistoric shore.

There's a secret as old
As the stones to unlock:
There are bones in the soil –
There's a child in the rock.
>   *It's a child,*
>   *It's a child,*
>   *It's a child,*   *Wind that brings iron and timber,*
>   *It's a child,*   *Takes sons, brings strangers,*
>   *It's a child.*   *Wind that fans the fire's hunger –*
>   *Whisper. Whisper. Who lives here?*

There's a longing, a promise,
The key to a spell:
There's a terrible choice
We are fated to fail.
    There's a choice,
    There's a choice,
    There's a choice,
    There's a choice,
    There's a choice.

Gentle sea hushing:

Good lordship, she's a quiet sea,
Slack tide an' a fair breeze
And nets a harrin'.

Bad lordship is a gale a wund,
The boat adrift or owertorned
And wrecken.

Hush, hush of sea.

Good lordship brings the shoowers an' sun
Tae swell the ear o' the corn
In hor right season.

Bad lordship is the nest awa',
The eggs smashed, the corbie craa'
Amang the clecken.

Hush of sea.

At the height of June it is barely night
For the blink of an eye. In the two a.m. twilight

The fields stir and wake.
                        Disembodied larks
Sing to each other in the dark,
Over the bent grass, under the stars;

First one, then many; invisible webs
Enmeshing the dunes like spider-threads
Embroidering the cool black air –

Messengers from another shore,
Close, and unreachable. Before

Dark solidifies into day,
The whole land holds its breath and waits,
Belonging neither to night nor morning.

Whir of wings.

Up on the height of its glorious hill,
The five-storey, silent, empty

Shell of the gatehouse floods and brims
With noise, gold, firelight, dancing;

And like an old heart that is tired of living,
That suddenly kindles with something like joy,

The hollow walls are brimful of music
The minstrels have come to the gallery.

Swallows singing inside gatehouse:

And the swallows are needles,
Blue-black arrows,

Ravelling breath-taking streamers of flight,
Making doors out of windows,
Effortless shadows,
Wreathing the castle in flickering light

Between silence and sunrise,
Darkness and daybreak,
Emptiness and music,

Between ecstasy and heartbreak.

Fade out swallows. Outside, distant kittiwakes:

There's a secret as deep
As the sea. In the dark
At the heart of the rock
There's a fault. There's a crack.
    There's a child,   *Sea that gives*
    There's a child,   *Salt and herring,*
    There's a child,   *Sea that bears*
    There's a child,   *The sun each morning,*
    There's a child.   *Sea that swallows*
                                      All its children –

Fade out kittiwakes.

                         Whisper. Whisper.
                           Who lives here?

An August night. Above the clouds
Over the Egyncleugh, the moon

Rises. The wind is slowing down,
The world relaxing into sleep.

Not a bird on the water. Only the hush
Of the long grass, and the sea's wash,

And the slightest stir of birds on the cliff –
A cleared throat, a chuckle, a cough:

A ship of sleepers cast adrift.
A crane-fly whirs. Papery moths,

Water-marked wings the colour of stone,
Drift through the thistles; and the moon,

Climbing, draws a path across
The darkening water; phosphorous

Catching the ripples as they run
In liquid silver, a seething shoal
Of scales and fire.

The castle walls
Loom higher in the dark, a great
Wrecked ship. The moon illuminates

Its cargo – feathery grasses, lichens,
Spokes of hogweed, may-crown plantains,

Daisies, studding the decks like stars.
Its brightness calls, and all light things answer.

In the courtyard, around the foundations,
The kitchens, the chapel, the Constable's chambers,

Leathery wings flit. Woodlice trundle,
Armour on stone. A spider trembles,

A web's bull's-eye in the moon's full glare.
On the arc of its journey, fierce white fire

Catches and fills a heart-shaped window.

And the deepest dark of the castle walls –
Doors going nowhere, hearths, holes,

Garderobes, stairways bent at odd angles –
Join with the wider dark, the miles

Of field and heugh, and wind-blown fell,

Millennia of dark, the men
And women lost beyond recall,

Absorbed in silence, earth and stone.

Oot a the neet
Wi'oot a soond,
Ower the heather
An' benty groond,
Ower the moors
An' ower the mosses,
Th' grab wor kye,
Th' steal wor hosses,

Th' raid wor hemmels
An' byres an' steeds
An' born wor hooses
Aboot wor heeds.

Th' come like the wund
Or the snaa' in June.
Th'll gollup the meat
For' off yee'r spoon.
Th'll tyek yee'r spindle,
Yee'r kist an' quern,
An' strip the blanket
For' off the bairn;
They'll whup the sark
For' off'n yee'r back,
Then trapple yee'r barley
An' fire yee'r stacks.

Th' bring nae baggage
An', when they've fled,
Leave nowt but widders
An' empty beds;
Empty bellies
An' hairts as sair
As fields a stubble
And esh. Aah sweer,
Though this be the country
God forgot,
The divvil receive
The reivin' Scot!

Eerie bird noises – curlew, oystercatchers.

The stones smell smoky. Bracken rusts
On the bank. Pools of mist

Make an island of the hill
Around the heugh. Along the wall,

Creeping deep, wet, soot-black stains
Darken the ashlar, streaked like flames.
Nettles blacken in the rain.

In garderobe, chimney, deep green gloom
Of low, cold-ceilinged sentry-rooms,

In fusty corners, upside down,
Shut butterflies have turned to stone.

Under the water-trough squats a toad.
Its squashy sides squeezing like bellows,

It stretches, blinks.

From somewhere high
And far and lifted up, a cry

Prickles the skin and stirs to flight –
A fear, a fire in the night,
A spark in tinder – catches light,

Till every living thing stiffens and stops
To listen.
Geese!
The chain unclasps

And fastens again in the watery sky.

Oxen, they brought, and sheep,
And the things they carried,

All they possessed on earth –
A blanket, a net, an axe –

Their cobles, crops, homes
Burned, and the wind harried

The smoke across the fields
From Little Mill to Brunton.

We herded them like sheep.
They slept in sheds, with oxen.

Then one night in the dark
We heard them softly singing:

The stories that we carry
Will not be burned or stolen;

The castle is an ark
That carries us to safety.

The stories that we carry
Will not be burned or stolen;

The castle is an ark
That carries us to safety.

Loud gust of wind. Inside tower:

There's a feud that is spread
On the wind by a word,
Like a spark in a stackyard,
A plague in the blood.
There's one law for some.
It's the way things are done.
Is it justice you seek?
It's a son for a son.

It gnaws at the heart
As a dog chews a skull,
Down the ladder of years
As the wind gnaws the sills;
As the sea grinds the shore
It deepens, grows old.
It's a refuge we seek
From the wind and the cold.

It's a statement of strength;
It's a threat; and to all
Who are blown with the thistledown
Over the fell,
It's an ark in a storm,
It's a shelter from harm,
It's a harbour, a haven,
A welcome home.
    It's a home,
    It's a home,
    It's a home,
    It's a home,
    It's a home.

A knife hilt. A belt tag. A stirrup. An ink well.
A penny. A pitcher. The bit from a bridle.
A tin spoon. A flagon. A bone comb. A bangle.
A glass bead. A button. A hinge and a spindle.

Th' bring nae baggage
                    Oot a the neet
                                        There's a feud that is spread
An', when they've fled,
                    Wi'oot a soond,
                                        On the wind by a word,
Leave nowt but widders
                    Ower the heather
                                        Like a spark in a stackyard,
An' empty beds;
            An' benty groond,
                                A plague in the blood.
Empty bellies
            Ower the moors
                            There's a feud that is spread
An' hairts as sair
                An' ower the mosses,
                                    On the wind by a word,
As fields a stubble
                Th' grab wor kye,
                                    Like a spark in a stackyard,
And esh. Aah sweer,
                Th' steal wor hosses,
                                    A plague in the blood.
Though this be the country
                Th' raid wor hemmels
                                    There's a feud that is spread
God forgot,
            An' byres an' steeds,
                                On the wind by a word,
The divvil receive
                An' born wor hooses
                                    Like a spark in a stackyard,
The reivin' Scot!
            Aboot wor heeds.
                            A plague in the blood.

Wind that brings iron and timber,
Takes sons, brings strangers,
Wind that fans the fire's hunger –
   Whisper. Whisper. Who lives here?

Advent. A visit. The hall,
The high table; the Earl
And starry retinue –
A hundred of them, or more,

Seated at table below.
Laughter, noise. The glow
And heat of a crackling fire
Roasting their cheeks; their shadows

Dancing on the wall
Weave and twine. The smell
Of gravy: rabbit, veal,
Steaming roast mutton and ale;

The rustling folds of their clothes,
Plum-coloured velvet and gold
Brocade, and bear-fur; the wool
Tapestries on the wall

Vivid with leaves and flowers,
Wreathes of ivy and rose;
On the rush-scattered floor, as still
As funerary stone,

The hunting dogs doze and dream
Of hot, salt blood on the tongue.
And listen: high overhead,
Rising above the hum

And clatter of voices –
High as the clouds of heaven
Over the Earl, the sun
Piercing the shadows – music:

Trumpet, pipe, drum.

And into the hall, in a flash, flies a sparrow,
Out of the dark of the western window,

Cold on its wings, its small heart racing,
Over the hundred heads, unnoticed,

Never pausing, not for a moment,
Not for an instant's rest or stillness,

The arc of its journey true as an arrow
Out of the hall through the eastern window

Into the all-embracing darkness.

Sea that gives salt and herring,
Sea that bears the sun each morning,
Sea that swallows all its children –
    Whisper. Whisper. Who lives here?

Outside. Wind and sea, loud:

It is snowing. First, a rattle –
Ice splinters; rose petals.

White fields, black scars:
Far fells disappear;

Heugh and hilltop hunker down;
Whin tangle, hawthorn;

Then the face of walls, the stone
Bleached with snow-flowers, feather-blown.

Beside the grange, a scarlet streak –
An oystercatcher's blood-red beak

The only coloured thing in sight,
As on the tops of walls, snow settles,

On the green between the bristles
Of the moss. The sea is metal,

Boiling, thunderous. The white
Gulls, whipped up, are flecks of ice,

Shattered from the breakers. Foam,
Sea-flung, fizzes on the snow.

Sudden burst of storm noise – very loud:

Sea, milk-white in the Egyncleugh:
Shape-shifter, twister. Two sides
Boil, *(Boom!)* a confluence
That cracks like cannon-fire,
Spits up, *(Crash!)* volcanic,
Smashes in beads of glass –

And there is a frozen moment of stillness –
Before it folds *(Ssssss),* falls back
Into itself, white silk, hissing,
Just as the next surge rushes, pressing
Forward, swells and plunges, crashing
(Sssssssssshhhhhhhhhh)
Over the black.

Storm noise subsides.
Far-off sea and one melancholy oystercatcher:

On King Henry's shore, a heap
Of filthy rags and bone – a sheep,

A shipwreck, trailing spars and rigging,
Beards of fleece and skin, the straggling

Seaweed streamers of its guts –
Rubber bands, ravelled mats –

Hang from its rafters, ribs and spine;
And round its forelegs tangle twine,

Fishing nets and bladderwrack.
It has begun the long road back

To element and mineral.

Its socket glares. A blue-black fly
Sizzles in its empty eye,

And in the clean, salt, cold sea wind
Among the stones, its jawbone grins.

Queen Margaret has come from France.
The wind blows, and the grass
Trembles before it. Ice
Cracks on the pools like glass.

Over Queen Margaret's Tower
Five white swans,
Straight and clean as arrows,
Head for the south. My friend,

Who can we trust? Whose word
Is neither ice nor grass
Nor the shifting wind?
Over the field in-bye,

Shadow under its wings,
Hunger in its belly,
A chestnut kestrel bends,
Its eye stitched to its prey.

Quiet sea:

The immense quiet of evening: things
Returning home.
Stone that was bone in the morning and gold at three
Is only stone.

Now the flat, slate sky is feathered
Like a pigeon's breast,
Lilac, fiery pink and smoky grey
And, in the west,

Over Alnwick Moor and Hedgeley, flags
Of crimson flame
Blaze up from Cheviot, turning
Rock-pools to bloodstains.

It's a job for a friend,
It's a word in your ear,
It's a favour returned,
It's a sweetener, my dear;
It's the way things are done
With a gift or a name,
It's a well-oiled machine:
It's the patronage game.
    It's a game,
    It's a game,
    It's a game,
    It's a game,
    It's a game.

It's the strong and the weak.
It's a favour, I fear;
And, behind a locked door,
It's a word in your ear.
It's the way things are done.
It's a safe house for some.
It's the way power speaks
From the mouth of a gun.
It's a bolt in your back
Or a knife to your neck.
Is it justice you seek?
You'll be lucky, my friend.

It's a job for a friend,
It's a word in your ear,
It's a favour returned,
It's a sweetener, my dear;
It's the strong and the weak.
It's a favour I fear,
And, behind a locked door,
It's a word in your ear.
It's the way things are done
With a gift or a name,
It's a well-oiled machine:
It's the patronage game.

Now the land grows dark.
Yellow lichen glows,
Fluoresces on the tops.
The square foundations hold
The silver of the sky
In gritty puddles, while
The colours slowly drown
And darken, and the stone
Sedimentary clouds
Ease up out of the west,
Layer on relentless layer.

Under the Iron Bar's
Black and broken crown,
The blonde grass in-bye
Burns with unearthly fire.
The first sharp star
Pricks the darkening sky
Above Queen Margaret's Tower
And the black gut below –
Above the ragged walls
That slant down to the sea.

Into the dark they sink
Like coals, slowly cooling.

And Longstone, miles away,   *Wind that brings*
Sweeps its glassy beam   *Iron and timber,*
Over the slant sea's   *Takes sons,*
Rig and furrow. Home   *Brings strangers,*
It calls the unnumbered gulls,   *Wind that fans*
Oaring over the waves,   *The fire's hunger–*
Threading between the shadows,   *Whisper. Whisper.*
Drawing their dark roads home.   *Who lives here?*
Round it wheels – the days,
The years – unravelling
The last light left on earth,
The silver of the sea.

                                  Whisper. Whisper.
                                  Who lives here?

Quiet, inside tower; whistling wind:

My job's to watch. I guard this gate.
All night I hear the sea's low roar
Deep in the Egyncleugh, the sore
Wind around the battlements.
This is a melancholy place.
Through every loophole, gaping pit
And arrow-slit, the cold wind blows,
And all we want from life is peace.
It's peace, lord.

Sometimes, when the fires are lit,
And we are bored with ale and dice,
And tired of squabbling and fights,
I doze, and dream:

                    A winter's night.
Hooves on the hill. Slant wind and sleet.
Who is it hammers at the door?
I draw the bolts. You fall inside,
Exhausted, aching just to sleep.
But no; not yet. For down a stair
Cut in the rock I lead you.

                    Now
Imagine the thing you most desire –
The deepest longing in you – lies
There, in the dark, just out of reach,
Calling you. You have a choice –
To shout for help, or face your fate,
Your future, and prepare to fight;
And every fibre of you knows,
To meet that longing, you must choose
Right. But you are tired, so tired...
The dark spins round...In every life
This moment comes.

                    And then I dream
I call three witnesses to speak:

Call the maker, the creator
Of the castle walls, the father
Of the lakes, the gates and harbour;
Call all his strength, his power: to match
His castle's high estate, to watch
And guard and govern – judge, deliver
Virtue here on earth, and measure
Truth against its glassy mirror.

Next, call the snow-flake spinner, sweeper
Over the sea, the shifter, shaper,
Stealer of sons, the twister, breaker,
Stone-scratcher, cloud-chaser –
Call the wind – destroyer, seeker.

What do you seek?
          I dreamed a city
Rose from a hill above the sea –
A hope, a pledge, a memory
Of hope, a ghost beneath a glass,
A shining prophecy of peace.
Its lakes, its slender towers – a high,
Right aim, a journey's end, a thing
So beautiful, you stop, and gasp, and stare.

I call the King.

          There is no answer.
Nothing. No one there.

                  There is war, there is peace.
                    In the intimate place
                      At the heart of the rock
            There's a fault. There's a crack.
                          There's a child,
                          There's a child,
                          There's a child,
                          There's a child,
                          There's a child.

I'm tired of dreams. What do I care
For dusty old romances here,
With little to eat and nothing to do   *There's a sword in the rock.*
But warm myself at the fire and wait   *There's a splinter of glass*
For news that never comes? God knows,   *In the heart. In the soul*
This is a melancholy place.   *There's a terrible choice –*
                  Is it peace? Is it peace? Is it peace?
                        Is it peace? Is it peace?

All night I watch this gate. I sit
And listen to the sea, the roaring
Wind, and think, when you are called
To choose, to speak, will you choose right?

And what I ask of <u>you</u> is this –
The king we killed – between that shining
City and these roofless walls,
Between that promise and the sword –
Tell me, which of them was his?

He could not give us what we need,
Though all we need on earth is peace.

It's peace, Lord.

Quiet.
Outside, dripping water syncopated with the stresses of the words:

From the bony stones of the rough sea-wall,
Regular as heart-beats, drips fall.

Drips gather, fatten, spill
Down the stairs of the stones, from inky wells

And glistening pools: in stuccoed rooms
And caves of lichen, flowers bloom;

In ferny forests, waterfalls;
And chandeliers in glittering halls –

And their almost inaudible, silvery sound
As the cracked stone thaws and the drops drip down,

Down, is the sound of a spell undone,
Rousing, waking frozen stone.

Fade up kittiwakes, far off:

There's a sword in the rock.
There's a splinter of glass
In the heart. In the soul
There's a terrible choice –
    Is it peace?
    Is it peace?
    Is it peace?
    Is it peace?
    Is it peace?

At the heart of the rock
There's a fault. There's a crack.
In the heart, in the soul
There's a splinter of glass.

There's a choice,
There's a choice,
There's a choice,
There's a choice,
There's a choice.

End kittiwakes.

From a hole in the seaward wall, a snail
Stretches its foreparts, eases its tail,

Oozing over the knobbly grain,
Smoothing the stone with its slimy trail.

Its skirts slacken under it. Stretching one eye
To examine a patch of leafy lichen,

It feels its way down a ribbon of silver,
Studded with seashells, ancient mortar,

Fossil of topshell, cowrie, lime
Sliding under it. Taking its time.

Its slow mouth working, its gluey strings
Trembling in the breeze like skin,

It slithers over root and stalk
And crevice, the sepulchral dark

Hollow of the sea wall, where
The empty shell's reoccupied –

Invisible creatures twitch inside
An alabaster palace, made

In a single movement, from the twist
Of its newel post to its silky lip,

And everything circular starts again.

Kittiwakes, with sea – active, noisy:

Waregoose, wullymint,
Mullymac an' kittiwake,
Tommy noddy, cuddy duck,
Tudelum an' gormer.

Deed tides, big tides,
Wullymint an' mullymac,
Come, Jack, shine the lowe,
Days is gettin' longer.

And the sky is stone:
A rook glides over
Stratified distances,
Deposits of silver;

Heugh, cliff,
Egyncleugh,
The land's slow slide
To the edge of water.

And the sky is streaming,
The silvered grass
Running away,
The light, racing:

Go sky,
Wind-blown
Cloud, sea.
Stay, stone.

Oven-red,
Sulphur-yellow,
Thunder-dark,
Flesh-sallow,

Wind-clawed,   Go, sky!
Storm-driven,
Field-furrowed,   Stay, stone!
Cloud-riven,

Pigeon-grey,
Sky-blown,
Sea-swept
Sandstone.

Skull-stone	*Oven-red*
Snake-stone	*Sulphur-yellow*
Face-stone	*Thunder-dark*
Fist-stone;	*Flesh-sallow,*
Barred and	*Wind-clawed*
Brindled	*Storm-driven*
Tiger-	*Field-furrowed*
Stripe-stone;	*Cloud-riven,*
Redwood	*Pigeon-grey*
Stained stone,	*Sky-blown*
Water-marked	*Sea-swept*
Grain stone;	*Sandstone:*
Biscuit and	*Go, sky –*
Bread-stone;	
River-bottom	*Stay, stone.*
Mud-stone;	
Ocean	*Oven-red*
Mountain	*Sulphur-yellow*
Map-of-the	*Thunder-dark*
World-stone;	*Flesh-sallow,*
Eye-socket	*Wind-clawed*
Knuckle-bone	*Storm-driven*
Field-furrow	*Field-furrowed*
Blown stone;	*Cloud-riven,*
Red-gold	*Pigeon-grey*
Honeycomb	*Sky-blown*
Bone-marrow	*Sea-swept*
Blood-stone.	*Sandstone.*

Sea that gives salt and herring,
Sea that bears the sun each morning,
Sea that swallows all its children –
    Whisper. Whisper. Who are we?

The stories that we carry
Will not be lost or stolen.
The castle is an ark
That carries us to safety.

Kittiwakes – fade out.

Glossary

Benty – rough grass

Clecken – brood of nestlings
Corbie craa' – carrion crow
Cuddy duck – St Cuthbert's duck, the eider

Deed tides – dead or neep tides

Egyncleugh – the rocky inlet directly beneath Dunstanburgh

Garderobe – latrine
Gollup – gobble
Gormer – cormorant

Harrin' – herring
Hemmels – open-fronted cow sheds
Heugh – rocky outcrop

Iron Bar – local name for the northwestern ('Lilburn') Tower

Kist – chest in which belongings were kept
Kye – cattle

Lowe – light. 'Jack-shine-the-lowe' was a children's name for the moon

Mullymac – fulmar

Queen Margaret's Tower – eastern tower, above Egyncleugh, named after Margaret of Anjou, wife of Henry VI

Sark – shirt
Steeds – steadings, farm buildings

Tommy noddy – puffin
Tudelum – any small sea bird, such as a knot or dunlin

Waregoose – barnacle goose
Wullymint – guillemot